Writing from Within

ALSO BY DANILO TAMBONE

Unleash Your Writing Potential with ChatGPT:
A Comprehensive Guide for Non-Fiction Authors

(To be published soon)

Beyond Your Story:
*Unleash Your Potential with the Hero's Journey
and the Inside-Out Understanding*

AI Foundations:
*Discover the World of Artificial Intelligence
and Begin Your Journey as an AI Whisperer*

DANILO TAMBONE

Writing from Within

UNLEASH YOUR CREATIVITY WITH THE INSIDE-OUT UNDERSTANDING

DEDICATION

To my loving family and friends,
whose unwavering support and encouragement
have been the foundation of my journey.

To the countless writers and artists
who have inspired me through their authenticity and imagination,
showing me the transformative power of self-expression.

To all those who embark on the journey of writing from within:
may you find your authentic voice, embrace your vulnerability,
and discover the incredible potential that lies in your connection
with the whole creation.

And finally, to the unending wellspring of inspiration
that resides within each of us,
reminding us of our innate wisdom, resilience,
and boundless creativity.

CONTENTS

INTRODUCTION

Welcome, fellow writer!

I'm so glad you've decided to join me on this journey of exploring the Inside-Out Understanding and how it can transform the way we approach our writing. You see, writing is a deeply personal and intimate process. We pour our thoughts, feelings, and experiences onto the page, hoping to make an impact on our readers. But sometimes, we find ourselves struggling with writer's block, self-doubt, and the ever-elusive search for inspiration.

That's where the Inside-Out Understanding comes in. It's not just a different perspective on life; it's an inner knowing that transcends our thoughts and stories. It opens us up to a deeper reality that continuously manifests itself, showing us that life simply is, neither good nor bad. When we relax into the flow and take action on the insights we get, everything becomes so much easier and fulfilling.

So, what exactly is the Inside-Out Understanding? In a nutshell, it's the realization that we are one single reality, one single Life, and that the perception of being separate is just an illusion of our minds. At its core, the Inside-Out Understanding is built on three fundamental principles: Mind, Consciousness, and Thought. We'll delve deeper into these principles in the next chapter, but for now, let's just say they provide a foundation for recognizing the immense power we hold within ourselves to shape our lives and our writing.

Now, you might be wondering what this has to do with writing. Well, as writers, we often face challenges that stem from our own thinking. We question our abilities, stress over finding the perfect words, and agonize over whether our work will resonate with others. But when we embrace the Inside-Out Understanding, we begin to see that our thoughts don't define us or our writing. Instead, they're simply a part of the creative process that we can learn to navigate more effectively.

Throughout this book, we'll explore various aspects of the writing process, from overcoming writer's block and tapping into the power of flow to cultivating inspiration from within and embracing vulnerability in our work. Along the way, I'll share personal anecdotes and insights that have helped me harness the power of the Inside-Out Understanding in my writing journey.

For example, when I first began writing, I was plagued by self-doubt. I questioned myself: Who am I to share my story? Will it be beneficial to anyone? Does it even matter? As I delved into the Inside-Out Understanding, I came to the realization that I was not a separate, limited self, struggling to resolve unbearable problems. Instead, I began sensing I was the One playing with this embodied form, and that realization allowed me to let go of the illusion of separation and embrace the wholeness of creation. I realized that sharing my story was not about *me*. If, by writing from within, I could find the key to pointing my readers to the whole Universe through my story and insights, that would be of service to others for embracing that same mystery. This insight kickstarted my writing process, enabling me to write from a place of connection and authenticity, and I haven't stopped since.

And don't worry, this won't be a dry, academic exploration of concepts. We'll approach these ideas through the lens of real-life experiences and relatable stories that demonstrate the practical application of the Inside-Out Understanding. After all, writing is about connecting with others, and what better way to do that than by sharing our own experiences?

I'm genuinely excited to share this journey with you. I've seen firsthand how the Inside-Out Understanding can transform not only our writing but also our lives. It's my hope that by the end of this book, you'll feel empowered and inspired to embrace the Inside-Out Understanding in your own writing journey, unlocking your true potential as a writer.

So, grab your favorite writing instrument, settle into a comfortable spot, and let's begin our adventure into the world of writing from within. The journey starts now!

HOW TO USE THIS BOOK

This book is designed to serve as a guide on your writer's journey, presenting techniques and practices that I've embraced throughout my life. While my current approach to writing is deeply rooted in the Inside-Out Understanding, the methods shared in this book have played a significant role in my growth both personally and as a writer, and may prove useful to you as well. Keep in mind that there is no one-size-fits-all approach to creativity; instead, consider experimenting with these techniques to see which resonate with you and facilitate a state of flow in your writing.

Ultimately, the goal is to notice the insights that come to you as you apply these methods, so that you no longer need to rely on any specific technique. Instead, you'll be able to tap into the creative flow and allow it to guide you in producing your best work. You may want to apply some of these techniques for a certain amount of time, and then come back to this book to see how your perception has shifted in the meantime.

At the end of each chapter, you'll find two sets of prompts designed to help you reflect on and apply the insights presented. The first set, titled **Exploring this Chapter's Topics**, encourages you to consider the chapter's content and how it relates to your own writing practice. The second set, **Writing from Within**, delves deeper into the foundations of the Inside-Out Understanding and asks you to examine how this awareness resonates with your personal journey. By engaging with these prompts, you'll plant seeds of insight that can help you get in tune with the universal wisdom inherent in the creative process.

Then, you'll find a couple of pages with **Space for Creation** where you can jot down the insights you get chapter by chapter.

As you embark on this transformative journey, remember that the true power of writing lies not in adhering to specific techniques or practices, but in allowing yourself to be guided by the creative flow. Embrace the wisdom of the Inside-Out Understanding, and let it illuminate your path as you explore, grow, and ultimately unleash your full potential as a writer. May this book serve as a valuable companion on your journey, offering inspiration, guidance, and encouragement to write from within.

CHAPTER 1

THE THREE PRINCIPLES AND THE WRITER'S MIND

In the Introduction, we briefly touched upon the three fundamental principles of the Inside-Out Understanding: Mind, Consciousness, and Thought[1]. Now, it's time to delve deeper into these principles and explore how they relate to our writing process. By understanding these core principles and their individual manifestations, we'll be better equipped to navigate the challenges and opportunities that arise in our journey as writers.

Universal Mind vs. Personal Mind

The first principle, Mind, represents the universal intelligence or life force behind all creation. It's the source of our innate wisdom, creativity, and resilience. In the context of writing, recognizing the presence of this Universal Mind allows us to tap into a wellspring of inspiration and ideas that goes far beyond our personal experiences. Have you ever been struck by a sudden insight or idea that seems to come out of nowhere? That's the power of Mind at work. As I embarked on my writing journey by embracing the Universal Mind, I discovered the boundlessness of my creativity and connected with the infinite intelligence that resides within us. Instead of feeling limited by my personal experiences, I saw the threads of a universal hero's journey beyond my story. This realization enabled me to write from a place of wholeness, allowing my true voice to shine through.

---

[1] The Three Principles were first articulated by Sydney Banks, a Scottish welder who had a profound insight in the early 1970s that led to a significant personal transformation. His ideas were initially shared through his talks and seminars, and later through his books, such as *The Missing Link, The Enlightened Gardener, The Enlightened Gardener Revisited,* and *Second Chance.*

Our personal mind, on the other hand, is the individual manifestation of the Universal Mind within us. It's the seat of our unique thoughts, emotions, and experiences. When we open ourselves up to the creative force of the Universal Mind, we can access a wealth of ideas and inspiration that can fuel our writing, while honoring our personal mind as the vessel through which we express our unique perspectives.

Universal Consciousness vs. Personal Consciousness

Consciousness is our ability to be aware of our thoughts, feelings, and experiences. It's the lens through which we perceive the world and our place in it. The Universal Consciousness refers to the collective awareness that unites all that is, while our personal consciousness is the individual level of awareness we each possess.

As writers, our level of personal consciousness plays a crucial role in how we interpret and convey our ideas on the page. For example, have you ever read something you wrote years ago and thought, "Wow, I can't believe I used to think that way!" That's because our level of consciousness is always evolving, shaping the way we perceive and understand the world around us. By being aware of our consciousness, we can bring greater depth and nuance to our writing, allowing our readers to connect with our work on a deeper level.

During my writing journey, I've experienced moments when my personal consciousness has expanded, enabling me to see beyond the limitations of my thoughts and beliefs. These moments of insight have profoundly influenced my writing, bringing new depths of understanding and connection to my work.

Universal Thought vs. Personal Thought

Thought is the creative energy that brings our ideas and experiences to life. It's the bridge between the formless world of Mind and the tangible reality of our everyday lives. The Universal Thought refers to the formless, creative potential that exists within the Universal Mind, while our personal thoughts are the specific ideas, beliefs, and interpretations we each hold within our personal mind.

In writing, our personal thoughts shape the words we choose, the stories we tell, and the emotions we evoke in our readers. But here's the thing: our thoughts are not the ultimate truth. They're simply a tool we use to make sense of the world and express ourselves. By recognizing that our thoughts don't define us or our writing, we can learn to let go of self-doubt, judgment, and fear, allowing our authentic voice to shine through.

Some Considerations on the Three Principles

Jack Pransky[2], one of the most renowned trainers, facilitators, and authors in the field of the Inside-Out Understanding, famously wrote that "the Three Principles are not a way of seeing the world; they are the way the world works, no matter how one sees the world.[3]" They are not a tool or a methodology; they are a description of how life and our human experience work.

Oftentimes, my coaching clients ask me: if they're not a tool, how does one use them in real life? Well, the same way you use the principle of gravity. You may not know the exact details of the underlying law of physics, but you see that gravity keeps you somehow stuck to the ground. Being aware of it, you may decide to move yourself by crawling, walking, or running; or cycling, skating, or driving a car. For sure, you won't find yourself floating in the air, unless you're on an airplane that counterbalances gravity with the propulsion of its engines and that deals with airflow with its wings. In the same way, being aware of the existence of the Three Principles and their implications on our lives

---

[2] https://insideoutunderstanding.com/

[3] Pransky, Jack, *Seduced by Consciousness: A Life with The Three Principles*, CCB Publishing, May 2017, https://www.amazon.com/Seduced-Consciousness-Life-Three-Principles/dp/1771433205

makes everything easier. The inner knowing of a larger Intelligence before the creation and interwoven with what is created lets us live with the awareness that everything is perfect, even when we don't notice it; Consciousness allows us to experience Life and be aware of being alive; Universal Thought turns acorns into oaks, and our individual thoughts turn wood into tables and chairs, and thought-created worlds into our perceived experience of life.

Once we are aware of them, we may conduct our lives appreciating that what we see is usually filtered and distorted through our thoughts, mind, and level of personal consciousness. The simple fact of being aware of this, helps us take our perceptions with a grain of salt and keeps us curious of what lies beyond the stories that we tell ourselves. Undisturbed by human thought, what waits for us is peace, wisdom, and love. Not something we may or should artificially create in our mind by using meditation or mindfulness techniques; rather, our natural state when we don't wander in our misconceptions. And of course, meditation and mindfulness may slow down our thoughts and let us see beyond their noise; but the magic is in how beautifully we're designed, not in the techniques we use to notice it.

Applying the Three Principles to the Writing Process

Now that we've explored the Three Principles and their individual manifestations, let's look at how they can help us navigate the writing process more effectively.

First and foremost, embracing the Inside-Out Understanding can help us overcome writer's block. When we recognize that our personal thoughts are simply part of the creative process, we can learn to observe them without judgment or fear. This allows us to step back, gain perspective, and access the innate creativity and wisdom of the Universal Mind. For example, I notice a profound difference in my writing when I let my thoughts guide the process and when, instead, I stay in sync with the Universal Mind. In the first case, I tend to struggle to find the right words and end up building labyrinthine sentences that are hard to grasp. In the second case, words flow smoothly, often without me even noticing, with a clarity and simplicity that surprises me every time. By recognizing that my thoughts are just part of the process, I am able to let go of my self-imposed pressure and judgment, and soon find myself effortlessly tapping into the creative flow of the Universal Mind.

Additionally, understanding the role of personal consciousness in our writing can help us develop a more authentic and resonant voice. By being aware of our evolving consciousness, we can bring greater depth and insight to our work, connecting with our readers on a deeper level.

As my personal consciousness has grown and evolved throughout my writing journey, I've noticed a shift in the way I approach my work. No longer do I try to force my writing to conform to my own or external expectations; instead, I focus on expressing my authentic Self and the unique insights that arise from my ever-evolving awareness.

Finally, by recognizing the power of personal thought, we can learn to let go of the self-doubt and judgment that often hold us back as writers. Instead of getting caught up in the ever-changing stream of our thoughts, we can trust in our innate creativity and resilience, allowing our true voice to emerge.

The Road Ahead

In the chapters ahead, we'll dive deeper into the practical application of the Inside-Out Understanding in various aspects of the writing process, from overcoming writer's block to cultivating inspiration and embracing vulnerability.

But for now, take a moment to reflect on the Three Principles and their individual manifestations and how being aware of them might influence your own writing journey. Remember, the power to transform your writing lies within you, and by embracing the Inside-Out Understanding, you can unlock your full potential as a writer.

Exploring this Chapter's Topics:

1. Reflect on your experiences with writer's block or self-doubt. How can the understanding of the Three Principles and their individual manifestations help you navigate these challenges in the future?

2. How has your level of personal consciousness evolved throughout your writing journey? Can you identify specific moments where your perspective shifted or your understanding deepened?

3. Consider the role of personal thought in your writing process. How can you cultivate a healthier relationship with your thoughts, allowing you to express yourself more authentically and freely?

Writing From Within:

1. Meditate on the Universal Mind and its connection to your creativity. Write a reflection on how this understanding resonates with your personal beliefs or experiences as a writer.

2. In your journal or in the *Space for Creation* that follows, describe a moment when you felt deeply connected to your personal consciousness while writing. How did this awareness influence your writing and creative expression?

3. Engage in a free-writing exercise to explore the transformative aspects of the Three Principles and their individual manifestations in your writing. Write without judgment or editing, allowing your inner voice to guide your thoughts and words on this topic.

Space for Creation

Chapter 2

OVERCOMING WRITER'S BLOCK WITH THE INSIDE-OUT UNDERSTANDING

Writer's block is a common challenge that many of us face at one point or another in our writing journey. It can manifest as a lack of ideas, difficulty putting thoughts into words, or an overwhelming sense of self-doubt. But the good news is, the Inside-Out Understanding can help us overcome this obstacle and get back to writing with confidence and ease.

Recognizing the Role of Thought in Writer's Block

The first step in overcoming writer's block is to recognize that it's often a product of our own thinking. When we get caught up in our thoughts and start to believe that they define us or our abilities, we can become paralyzed by fear, doubt, and uncertainty.

But remember, our thoughts are simply part of the creative process, and they don't define us or our writing. By recognizing this, we can learn to observe our thoughts without judgment and allow them to come and go without getting stuck in a mental quagmire.

Shifting Our Perspective

When we're stuck in the throes of writer's block, it can be helpful to shift our perspective and remind ourselves of the bigger picture.

For example, instead of focusing on the perceived "problem" of writer's block, I stay curious and notice what the whole situation is about. Rather than seeing it in a different way, like labeling it as an "opportunity" instead of a "problem," I notice what my thoughts and feelings are telling me about it.

Am I questioning myself? My ability as a writer to convey my thoughts and insights in a meaningful way? Whether or not the readers will get me? Am I struggling to find the right words and metaphors? Am I even unclear about the point I want to make?

Writing is always an exploration, even when we feel confident about the subject. We continually see things afresh and may find that the words and metaphors we used in the past no longer fit our current level of consciousness. And that's okay. Exploring new territory means being prepared for surprises and remaining in awe of what comes next. I see that when I stay in this place of contemplation, words and metaphors come to me without even searching for them. Instead, when I try to force them, inevitably my personal mind tries to make sense of something I don't know yet, and I get stuck in the process. Paradoxically, writer's block could be a signal that we are on our path to discovering something new, and we can start to see it as a natural part of the journey rather than an insurmountable obstacle.

In the next paragraphs, we'll explore a couple of ways to restart the writing process and let go of writer's block. However, my experience tells me that without the awareness of what the block is about, "doing things" will help only until the next roadblock is encountered. So, remember to gently return to the Source and view the larger picture from there.

Tuning into the Universal Mind

As we mentioned earlier, the Universal Mind is the source of our innate wisdom and creativity. By getting in sync with this creative force, we can access a wellspring of ideas and inspiration that can help us overcome writer's block.

Did you notice I didn't use the phrase "connect with" the Universal Mind? The reason is, I don't see anything to connect. You connect parts that are separated. You connect two mechanical parts with a joint.

When you break something, you may try and connect back the fragments with glue. But when the separation from the Source is just an illusion, how do you connect with it? You don't. There's nothing to connect, only something to notice – our thoughts of separation, so deeply rooted into our mind that we don't even question them.

I'm not here to convince you about it. My experience so far is that this is not something our personal mind can grasp. It goes beyond definitions, concepts, ideas. It isn't a philosophy, even though I saw it described in metaphors in every spiritual tradition with which I came in touch. As we move into this exploration, I invite you to stay open to the possibility that Life is so much more that this transient thing we are accustomed to consider. Much more than black or white, right or wrong, here or there, me or them. Notice what you can notice and be prepared to get sudden insights where finally everything makes sense. And then, when you least expect them, other sudden insights will take your consciousness one step further, and then once more. And, once you see, you can't "unsee."

So, how do we connect with the Universal Mind? We don't. From what I see, we're already one with it, yet our personal minds may wander in the illusion of separation. Therefore, we don't "connect" with the Mind, but rather get back in sync with it. One way that I found useful is through practices like meditation, mindfulness, or simply taking a quiet moment to tune into our inner wisdom, as in the "Take 5" exercise that I describe in the closing prompts of this chapter (which is the only "practice," if we can call it that way, that I continue applying sometimes nowadays). Another approach is to engage in activities that spark our creativity and bring us joy, such as reading, listening to music, dancing, or going for a walk in nature. And once you become aware of your oneness, you may find yourself living more and more from a meditative state, without needing techniques to get there. By nurturing our attunement with the Universal Mind, we can tap into a seemingly endless source of inspiration and creative energy.

Taking Action

Sometimes, the best way to overcome writer's block is simply to start writing. This may seem counterintuitive, especially when we're feeling stuck, but taking action can help us break free from the mental barriers that are holding us back.

Set aside any judgments or expectations you may have about your writing and just start putting words on the page. It doesn't have to be perfect, and it doesn't even have to make sense. The important thing is to get the creative juices flowing and build momentum. You might be surprised at how quickly your writer's block begins to dissolve once you start taking action.

For example, when I began writing my first book *Beyond Your Story*, I created blog posts on my website, one for each chapter. Instead of questioning myself whether they were good enough to be published, or if they had the right structure, or language, or style, I simply went on writing and posting. As I did so, each chapter allowed me to explore the core concepts I wanted to share as well as different structures and styles, until I found the format that best resonated with my message. And finally, when I turned them into the actual book's chapters, I had enough experience and examples to turn those drafts into proper parts of a book, also supported by my Editor. The point is, I didn't let myself be overwhelmed by analysis paralysis, and the book basically took form without me even noticing. It was as if I had spent my entire life making experiences and gathering material, and now it was time to put the pieces of the puzzle on the table and let some universal forces connect the dots. Instead of getting stuck into self-doubts about what being a writer could mean and if I had the stuff to be one, I simply allowed myself playing with writing and let the creative flow take the lead.

The Road Ahead

In the following chapters, we'll continue to explore the practical application of the Inside-Out Understanding in various aspects of the writing process. We'll dive into topics like tapping into the power of flow, cultivating inspiration from within, and embracing vulnerability in our work. As we journey together through this understanding, keep in mind that the power to overcome writer's block – and any other challenges you may encounter – lies within you. Embrace the Inside-Out Understanding, and watch as your writing journey unfolds with newfound ease and joy.

Exploring this Chapter's Topics:

1. Reflect on your previous experiences with writer's block. Can you identify any patterns or common triggers that contribute to these moments of feeling stuck?

2. How have you tried to overcome writer's block in the past? Which strategies were effective, and which ones were less helpful?

3. Consider writer's block and your perspective on it. What are your thoughts and feelings telling you about it? How may these insights serve you in changing your approach to dealing with it?

Writing From Within:

1. I learned this "Take 5" exercise from Transformative Coach Michael Neill. Set aside 5 minutes for a quiet practice to tune into the Universal Mind. Simply stay at your desk or in a comfortable chair in a quiet place with no distractions for 5 minutes straight. Close your eyes if you like. No need to visualize anything, no mantra, no expectations. Just stay silent and notice what you notice. See your thoughts come and go. Sense your body's urge to move away, and gently remain where you are. Scratch your nose if you have to, but stay there. It's just 5 minutes. Afterward, journal about your experience. You may have struggled with your thoughts for the whole session, and that's okay. Insights or creative ideas may have emerged during

this time, and that's okay. You may not have seen or heard anything, and that's okay too. Try to do this once every day for a week, and then reflect on your experience. If you find it useful, you may continue as long as you want, or do it anytime you need to stay centered and grounded.

2. Create a list of activities that help you feel inspired and in tune with your inner wisdom. Experiment with engaging in at least one of these activities the next time you face writer's block.

3. Write a letter to yourself to read when you're experiencing writer's block. In this letter, remind yourself of the Inside-Out Understanding and offer words of encouragement and wisdom to help you overcome this challenge.

Space for Creation

CHAPTER 3

UNLOCKING YOUR AUTHENTIC VOICE

Your authentic voice is the unique writing style that reflects your true self, your experiences, and your perspective on the world. When you write with authenticity, your work resonates with readers, allowing them to connect with you and your message on a deeper level. In this chapter, we'll explore strategies for unlocking your authentic voice, as well as how the Inside-Out Understanding can help you develop authenticity in your writing.

Discovering Your Unique Writing Style

Developing your unique writing style is an ongoing process, requiring reflection, experimentation, and a willingness to embrace your individuality. I found the magic when, through my inner journey, I discovered a spark leading me beyond my smaller self and into the realm of the universal. I realized that our unique voice is not merely the style we use to convey thoughts and insights; instead, it is the channel through which we guide readers from their self-doubt to universal realizations that resonate with them, making them feel heard and seen.

Here are some steps to help you discover your authentic writing voice:

- *Reflect on your values, beliefs, and experiences:* Consider what is most important to you and how your experiences have shaped your perspective on the world. Use these insights as a foundation for your writing, infusing your work with your personal truths. I already mentioned that I began writing to share my spiritual beliefs and my journey from feeling separate to sensing my interconnectedness with the whole creation. Once I allowed myself to incorporate these insights into my work, I found that my writing became more authentic and relatable.

- *Read widely and analyze the writing styles of authors you admire:* By exposing yourself to diverse voices and styles, you can gain a better understanding of what resonates with you and what you want to incorporate into your own writing. I've always been drawn to authors who write with an engaging, inspiring, and accessible style, and who share personal stories and anecdotes to illustrate their points, making their content relatable to readers. Their influence has helped shape my own writing voice.

- *Experiment with different writing techniques and formats:* As you write, try out different techniques, such as varying sentence structures, using unique metaphors, or experimenting with various narrative perspectives. This process of exploration will help you discover the writing style that suits you best.

How the Inside-Out Understanding Can Help You Develop Authenticity in Your Writing

The Inside-Out Understanding teaches us that our thoughts and feelings shape our experiences and that we have an innate wellspring of wisdom and creativity within us. By tapping into this inner resource, we can develop a more authentic writing voice that reflects our true selves.

Here are some ways the Inside-Out Understanding can help you cultivate authenticity in your writing:

- *Let go of self-imposed limitations:* By embracing the Inside-Out Understanding, you can recognize the illusory nature of the separate self and let go of the layers that confine your true expression. This honest and vulnerable approach will resonate with readers, helping you create more meaningful connections through your writing. My journey from an ego-driven perspective to embracing the mystery of the unspeakable has allowed me to share my experiences, both the struggles and the insights, with readers who can relate to my story.

- *Trust your inner wisdom:* As you write, trust that your inner wisdom will guide you towards your authentic voice. Instead of seeking external validation or trying to conform to your own or other people's expectations, listen to your own intuition and let it guide your writing. When I learned to trust my inner voice, I found that my writing became more genuine and impactful.

- *Overcome self-doubt and fear:* The Inside-Out Understanding can help you recognize that self-doubt and fear are simply transient thoughts that do not define you or your writing. By acknowledging and releasing these limiting beliefs, you can write with greater freedom and authenticity. This has been instrumental in my own writing journey, as it has allowed me to overcome the barriers that once held me back.

The Road Ahead

As you continue to develop your authentic writing voice, remember that it is an ongoing journey of discovery and growth. Embrace the Inside-Out Understanding, and trust that your unique voice will emerge as you continue to explore your inner world and share your truth with the world through your writing.

Exploring this Chapter's Topics:

1. Reflect on your personal values, beliefs, and experiences. How do these aspects of your life influence your writing and the messages you want to convey?

2. List three authors whose writing styles you admire. Identify specific elements of their styles that resonate with you and consider how you might incorporate these elements into your own writing.

3. Describe your current writing style. What are its strengths, and what aspects would you like to develop further?

Writing From Within:

1. Set aside 20 minutes for a freewriting exercise. Write without stopping, focusing on expressing your thoughts and feelings as honestly and openly as possible. Afterward, review your writing and identify any patterns or themes that emerge, reflecting on how your insights inform your authentic voice.

2. Write a short piece of fiction or creative nonfiction that reflects your personal values, beliefs, or experiences. Experiment with different narrative perspectives, sentence structures, or metaphors, and note which techniques feel most authentic to you, from the inside-out.

3. Reflect on a time when you experienced self-doubt or fear in your writing process. How did these feelings affect your writing, and how might the Inside-Out Understanding help you overcome these obstacles in the future? As you consider this question, remember that the Inside-Out Understanding can empower you to let go of limiting beliefs and embrace your authentic writing voice with confidence and grace.

Space for Creation

CHAPTER 4

TAPPING INTO THE POWER OF FLOW

Flow is a state of deep immersion, focus, and enjoyment in an activity, often resulting in heightened creativity and productivity. When you enter a flow state while writing, you become fully absorbed in your work, allowing your words to flow effortlessly and your ideas to come together seamlessly. In this chapter, we'll explore the concept of flow in the context of writing and share practical tips for entering and maintaining a flow state while writing. I will also share my personal journey of discovering flow and how it transformed my writing experience.

Understanding the Concept of Flow in the Context of Writing

Flow, a term coined by psychologist Mihaly Csikszentmihalyi[4], describes a state of complete absorption in an activity characterized by intense focus, enjoyment, and a sense of timelessness. In the context of writing, flow is often associated with periods of heightened creativity, productivity, and a deep connection with one's inner wisdom and authentic voice. When you enter a flow state, your inner critic recedes into the background, allowing your ideas and words to unfold naturally and with ease.

Writers who consistently experience flow often report not only increased productivity and creative output but also a greater sense of satisfaction and fulfillment in their work.

---

[4] Csikszentmihalyi, Mihaly, *Flow: The Psychology of Optimal Experience*, Harper Perennial Modern Classics, 1st edition, July 1, 2008, https://www.amazon.com/Flow-Psychology-Experience-Perennial-Classics/dp/0061339202

I have no memory of how one of the most inspired pieces of my book *Beyond Your Story* came to life. I wanted to share my personal insights about one of the stages of Joseph Campbell's Hero's Journey, *Master of the Two Worlds*, and I knew it was a tough one. It's the part when the Heroes, after a profound transcendental experience that made them lose their past identity and totally shifted their perception on life, return to their ordinary world and share insights with their people. Their challenge, now, is to find words to explain what they went through, with the awareness that words can't match the mystery of the unspeakable they experienced. That was the exact challenge I was expecting to find on my way. So, I simply relaxed, took my 5 minutes to detach from the thoughts telling me how hard it would be expressing my insights about it, and began writing. The writing act took around 10 minutes in total. I was astonished at both the depth and the clarity of the message that had just taken form in front of me, as well as the choice of words. Simple, but not so simple to steer away from its deep meaning. Deep, but not so deep to sound enigmatic and inaccessible. I didn't even have to review any words or sentences, and the final form that paragraph has in the book is the same in which it was generated. Pure inspiration, pure flow.

Practical Tips for Entering and Maintaining a Flow State While Writing

The Inside-Out Understanding leads us to the insight that flow is an inner game rather than a state induced by external factors. In the example above, I can't recall any specific tricks I used to ignite the flow, except for being present and not carried out by my rambling thoughts.

On the other hand, along my journey I found some useful practices to create basic conditions and encourage flow while writing:

- *Minimize distractions:* Designate a quiet and clutter-free writing space where you can fully concentrate on your work. Turn off notifications on your devices and consider using apps or tools to block distracting websites during your writing sessions.

- *Discover how your biorhythms work:* Notice if there are moments in the day when your writing flows more easily. For me, early mornings work better for rational tasks like reviewing and editing, while late afternoons (during the weekend) and evenings (after office hours during the workweek) seem to be perfect for my creative writing.

- *Set clear goals and intentions:* Before you begin writing, establish clear objectives for your session, such as completing a certain number of words or a specific section of your project. Having a clear sense of direction can help you maintain focus and momentum.

- *Warm up with a pre-writing routine:* Engage in a pre-writing routine, such as free-writing, brainstorming, or outlining, to help you transition into your writing session and spark your creativity. I often begin my writing sessions with a *Take 5* to center myself and tap into my inner wisdom.

- *Practice mindfulness and presence:* As you write, stay present and fully engaged in the task at hand. If your mind begins to wander or you find yourself becoming self-critical, simply notice those thoughts, acknowledge them as clouds in your mind and not as real things, and return to the page. Notice how the Flow is "using you" to turn creative potential into written words, and surrender to it. This practice has helped me to let go of self-doubt and embrace my authentic voice.

- *Allow for flexibility and spontaneity:* While it's important to have a plan and clear goals, be open to the natural flow of ideas and creative inspiration as you write. Give yourself permission to deviate from your outline or explore new directions as they arise. I am often surprised of the unexpected turns my writing takes even when I think I know what to write. Sudden insights come up as I type, and I simply follow the flow. The results are often more inspiring than the ones I had in mind.

- *Take breaks and recharge:* Regular breaks may be useful for maintaining focus and energy during your writing sessions. Notice if stepping away from your work for a few minutes to stretch, taking a walk, or engaging in another rejuvenating activity helps sustain your flow state. On the other hand, if you see your creative flow pouring out freely, you may want to avoid breaking it until your cup is empty and recharge after that.

Be mindful that we tune into the flow when we stop disturbing it with our wandering mind. For what I see, we don't need to *do something* to tap into it, but rather *do less* of the things that block it. Therefore, the practices above can help us reduce the inner noise and stay receptive as our insights choose the right words to take form on the page. Rather than spending all your effort on being super-disciplined in using any combination of the practices above, I advise you to stay curious of how your inner game shifts as you apply them. That's the state you'll want to be in more and more.

Ultimately, by incorporating these strategies or any other ones that free your reins into your writing practice or going beyond any techniques and tuning into your inner presence, you'll tap into the power of flow, allowing you to write with increased creativity, productivity, and enjoyment. As you continue to cultivate flow in your writing, you'll find that your relationship with your work deepens, and you'll be better able to access your inner wisdom and authentic voice.

The Road Ahead

As you embark on your journey to tap into the power of flow, remember that it's a continuous process, with its rises and falls. Be patient. Bless the productive moments when your thoughts support the creative flow. Bless the apparently unproductive moments when you notice your thoughts blocking it. Recharge when you sense it's time to fill up your cup. Embrace the strategies shared in this chapter and trust that, over time, you will develop the ability to enter and maintain a flow state with greater ease, ultimately enhancing your creativity and connection with your authentic voice.

Exploring this Chapter's Topics:

1. Reflect on your current writing environment. What distractions might be hindering your ability to enter a flow state? Identify specific changes you can make to minimize these distractions.

2. Describe a time when you experienced a flow state while writing. What factors do you think contributed to this experience? How can you recreate these conditions in future writing sessions? Was it more of an external or an inner game?

3. Choose one or more of the practical tips from this chapter and start incorporating them into your writing routine. After a week, evaluate whether these changes have had a positive impact on your ability to enter and maintain a flow state.

Writing From Within:

1. Before your next writing session, set a clear goal or intention for your work. As you write, stay focused on this objective, and notice whether this sense of direction helps you maintain a flow state or if it rather disturbs it by adding self-expectations. Adjust consequently.

2. Experiment with different pre-writing routines, such as free-writing, brainstorming, or outlining. After each exercise, take note of how it impacts your ability to enter a flow state during your writing session. Then, let you inner knowing guide you to tap into that flow state, with or without these techniques.

3. During your next writing session, surrender to your writing. Let it tell you how it wants to be written. Don't drive, don't guide. Put yourself at the service of a creativity that wants to flow through you, exactly as you are. Your experiences, your story, your skills, your study, your research – all of them collide here and now in one single whole, in what you are right now, without effort. No need to demonstrate how well you did so far, how

much you're committed to this right now, and how capable you are of exceptional results. Simply notice how you *are used* by creativity to turn the flow into written words. Enjoy the ride.

Space for Creation

CHAPTER 5

EMBRACING THE UNKNOWN: THE ROLE OF UNCERTAINTY IN THE WRITING PROCESS

As writers, we often encounter uncertainty throughout our creative journeys. Learning to embrace the unknown and navigate it with the Inside-Out Understanding can help us find our way and foster our growth as writers. In this chapter, we'll discuss the importance of embracing uncertainty and how the Inside-Out Understanding can guide us through the unknown aspects of the creative process.

The Inevitability of Uncertainty in Writing

Uncertainty is an inevitable part of the writing process. Whether we're starting a new project, revising a draft, or seeking feedback, we're often faced with questions, doubts, and unknowns. This uncertainty can be uncomfortable, but it can also serve as a catalyst for growth and discovery. By embracing the unknown, we can develop resilience, flexibility, and adaptability, essential qualities for thriving as writers.

Embracing Uncertainty with the Inside-Out Understanding

The Inside-Out Understanding can offer valuable insights into navigating uncertainty in our writing. Here are a few key principles to keep in mind:

- *Trust your inner guidance:* Rely on your intuition and inner wisdom when faced with uncertainty. They can serve as powerful guides, helping you make decisions and move forward with confidence.

- *Recognize the role of thought:* Remember that our feelings of uncertainty often arise from our thoughts. By acknowledging the transient nature of thoughts, we can learn to let go of unhelpful doubts and anxieties, making space for inspiration and creativity.

- *Stay present:* Focus on the present moment, rather than getting lost in future worries or past regrets. Being present can help you stay grounded and open to new insights and ideas, even amid uncertainty.

- *Be flexible and adaptable:* Embrace change and be willing to adjust your plans, expectations, or even your writing style as needed. By remaining open and adaptable, you can navigate the unknown with greater ease and grace.

- *Cultivate patience:* Recognize that the writing process takes time, and it's natural to encounter uncertainty along the way. Practice patience and trust that clarity will emerge as you continue to write and explore.

Practical Tips for Embracing Uncertainty in Writing

Here are some practical tips for embracing uncertainty in your writing journey:

- *Set intentions rather than rigid goals:* Instead of focusing on specific outcomes, set intentions for your writing, such as connecting with your authentic voice, exploring new ideas, or pushing your creative boundaries.

- *Experiment and play:* View uncertainty as an opportunity for creative exploration. Try new writing techniques, styles, or genres, and see where your curiosity takes you.

- *Seek support and community:* Surround yourself with other writers and creatives who can offer encouragement, feedback, and camaraderie. Sharing your uncertainties and experiences with others can help you gain new perspectives and insights.

- *Go easy on yourself:* Be kind and understanding with yourself as you navigate uncertainty. Acknowledge the challenges and difficulties of the writing process, and remember that every writer faces their own unique uncertainties.

- *Reflect on your growth:* Regularly take the time to reflect on your writing journey, acknowledging the uncertainties you've faced, the insights you've gained, and the growth you've experienced.

Summary

Embracing uncertainty is a crucial aspect of the writing process. By applying the Inside-Out Understanding and adopting a flexible, open, and patient mindset, you can navigate the unknown with confidence and grace. Remember that uncertainty is an opportunity for growth and discovery, and trust in your inner guidance to lead you through the creative journey.

Exploring this Chapter's Topics:

1. Reflect on your experiences with uncertainty in your writing journey. How have you navigated these unknowns in the past, and how can you apply the Inside-Out Understanding to embrace uncertainty more effectively in the future?

2. Consider a time when you faced a significant uncertainty in your writing. What lessons or insights did you gain from that experience? How can you apply those lessons to future writing projects?

3. Identify one or more areas of uncertainty in your current writing project. How can you apply the principles and practical tips discussed in this chapter to embrace and navigate this uncertainty?

Writing From Within:

1. Reflect on your personal experiences with the Inside-Out Understanding. How is this awareness influencing your writing process and the way you approach uncertainty? Write a journal entry or personal essay detailing your thoughts, experiences, and any insights you've gained through embracing the unknown in your writing.

2. Choose a specific writing project or idea that is currently shrouded in uncertainty for you. Using the Inside-Out Understanding as a guide, explore the unknown elements of this project and write a short piece describing how embracing this uncertainty is leading you to new insights, growth, and creative breakthroughs.

3. Develop a mindfulness practice that encourages you to tap into your inner wisdom and insights when facing uncertainty in your writing journey. This can be a daily meditation, journaling, or contemplative walking routine, or simply staying present with a *Take 5*. Focus on cultivating a deep connection with your inner guidance system and remaining open to the wisdom that arises in the moment when you need it most. Reflect on how this practice supports you in navigating challenges, doubts, or unknown elements in your writing projects, and consider how it helps you stay connected to the Inside-Out Understanding.

Space for Creation

CHAPTER 6

CULTIVATING INSPIRATION FROM WITHIN

Inspiration is a vital component of the creative writing process, fueling your ideas and giving life to your words. While it's common to seek external sources of inspiration, it's equally important to open up your inner source of inspiration by tapping into your intuition and insight. In this chapter, I'll share my personal journey of learning to cultivate inspiration from within, exploring the role of intuition and insight in the creative process, and sharing the breakthroughs I've discovered along the way.

The Role of Intuition and Insight in the Creative Process

Intuition refers to the ability to understand or know something without conscious reasoning, while insight is a sudden, deep understanding of a complex problem or situation. Both intuition and insight play crucial roles in the creative writing process, helping you generate original ideas, make connections between seemingly unrelated concepts, and uncover the deeper meaning and significance in your work.

By learning to trust and access your intuition and insight, you can enhance your creativity, develop a more authentic writing voice, and create work that resonates with your readers on a deeper level.

Techniques for Opening Up to Your Inner Source of Inspiration

Cultivating inspiration from within may require practice, awareness, and a willingness to explore your inner world. Oftentimes, we block the flow of inspiration with self-conscious thoughts about what we think is right or wrong, whether we deserve to experience it or not, or if we are prepared enough to commit to becoming a writer. It's our inner trouble-creation game and is not inherent into the creative act per se. You see, our little mind operates with the sets of data it has accrued from the past and can be super useful when dealing with repetitive and standard tasks. The problem comes when we use it to predict the future or to create something new, both of which require opening up to the unknown and becoming comfortable with staying into it. There, our rational mind can still support us with trends coming from past data to provide a direction. However, I sense that the beauty of the creative act lies in keeping those indications in mind while setting ourselves free to explore the unknowable, allowing our intuition to guide us and balancing personal thought and inner wisdom.

Here are some techniques that I found useful on my writing journey for opening up to our inner source of inspiration:

- *Engage in mindfulness practices:* Mindfulness practices, such as meditation, deep breathing exercises, or journaling, can help you quiet your mind and tap into your inner wisdom, creating ideal conditions for inspiration to emerge. Then, if you feel that these outside-in practices become additional burdens that distract you from the creative process, return to the *Take 5*, and notice what you have to notice.

- *Embrace your emotions and experiences:* Our emotions and experiences are a rich source of inspiration for our writing. Instead of avoiding or suppressing your feelings, allow yourself to fully experience and express them through your work, creating a deeper connection with your readers.

- *Trust your intuition:* As you write, learn to trust your intuition and follow its guidance. Allow your instincts to lead you in your writing, even if it means deviating from your original plan or exploring new ideas that arise unexpectedly.

- *Cultivate curiosity and open-mindedness:* Adopt an attitude of curiosity and open-mindedness, both in your writing and in your daily life. Explore new topics, engage in diverse experiences, and seek out fresh perspectives to fuel your creativity and inspire your writing.

- *Reflect on your dreams and subconscious thoughts:* Your dreams and subconscious thoughts can be a treasure trove of inspiration, revealing hidden insights and creative ideas. Keep a dream journal or practice techniques like free association to access and explore the wisdom of your subconscious mind.

- *Be patient and kind to yourself:* Cultivating inspiration from within may take time and patience. Be kind to yourself as you navigate the ups and downs of the creative process, trusting that your inner wisdom and inspiration will reveal themselves in their own time. For me, it's been the very act of writing that ignited my intuition and the creative flow, together with noticing that the less I put my mental boundaries into what I write, the more fluidly my insights take form.

The Road Ahead

As you embark on your own journey to cultivate inspiration from within, remember to be patient with yourself and trust the process. By opening up to your inner source of inspiration, you'll tap into the wellspring of creativity, intuition, and insight that lies within you. As you continue to develop your writing practice and embrace the Inside-Out Understanding, you'll find that your work becomes more authentic, inspired, and fulfilling, reflecting the unique wisdom and perspective that only you can offer.

Exploring this Chapter's Topics:

1. Reflect on a time when you felt particularly inspired while writing. What do you think sparked this inspiration? Was it more of an outside-in or inside-out experience? My journey

from feeling separate to acknowledging our wholeness, and my desire to share this insight with the world, have been significant sources of inspiration for me.

2. Consider your current writing routine. Are there any practices or habits you can adopt to help you cultivate inspiration from within? Identify specific changes you can make to your routine to open up to your inner source of inspiration.

3. Discuss a recent experience or emotion that deeply affected you. How can you use this experience or emotion as inspiration for your writing?

Writing From Within:

1. Choose one of the techniques from this chapter to open up to your inner source of inspiration, and practice it regularly for two weeks. As you do that, reflect on how this practice is impacting your writing and your sense of inspiration. Then, if and when you sense it's the right time, experiment with embracing your intuition without following any strict practices. For me, noticing that peace is what I am made of, not an inner state to recreate, and that I see it more clearly when my mind is undisturbed by rambling thoughts, has made a significant difference.

2. During your next writing session, practice trusting your intuition by allowing it to guide your writing. This may involve deviating from your original plan or exploring new ideas that arise unexpectedly. Afterward, reflect on how this intuitive approach affected your writing and your sense of inspiration. My own experience has shown me that trusting my intuition can lead to unexpected and rewarding discoveries in my writing.

3. Engage in an activity or experience outside of your usual routine, such as attending a workshop, visiting a new place, or trying a new creative medium. Reflect on how this experience

influenced your perspective and inspired your writing. Oftentimes, by stepping out of my comfort zone and forging new mental connections, I've found new sources of inspiration and gained fresh insights that have enriched my writing.

Space for Creation

CHAPTER 7

WRITING AS A TRANSFORMATIVE JOURNEY

Writing is not only an act of creation but also a transformative journey of personal growth, inner discovery, and authentic expression. As you navigate the writing process, you have the opportunity to delve into your inner world, explore your thoughts and emotions, and develop a deeper understanding of yourself and your place in the world. In this chapter, we'll discuss the transformative aspects of writing, highlighting personal growth and the importance of embracing vulnerability and inner discovery in the writing process.

Personal Growth Through Writing

Writing can be a powerful catalyst for personal growth, providing you with opportunities to:

1. *Develop awareness:* Writing allows you to reflect on your thoughts, feelings, and experiences. It fosters a deeper understanding of yourself and your personal narrative. I see that the real magic happens when, starting from there, you take the chance to transcend your story and connect with its underlying universal threads. Your writing stops being only about you, connects with the essence of what we are, and touches the inner chords in you and your audience.

2. *Cultivate empathy and compassion:* Writing about the experiences and perspectives of others can help you develop empathy and compassion, expanding your understanding of the human experience. That's what I saw when I guided Jennifer and Gisela on their Hero's Journeys for *Beyond Your Story* and then turned into short stories the dialogues I had with them. Seeing the world through their eyes, gently touching their souls as they opened their

hearts, and being a witness to the insights they found along the way was a humbling and awakening experience for me.

3. *Enhance critical thinking and problem-solving skills:* The process of organizing your thoughts, developing arguments, and exploring ideas through writing can sharpen your critical thinking and problem-solving abilities. I notice that sometimes I may not have all the answers I need on a specific topic in advance, but the very act of writing helps me summon insights and put the puzzle's pieces together.

4. *Build resilience and perseverance:* Navigating the challenges of the writing process can help you develop resilience, perseverance, and the ability to overcome obstacles. It requires a delicate balance between the creative act, where intuition and flow are paramount, and the editing part, where the rational mind helps spot incongruences and supports in refining your work. It's a dance where music and rhythm change often, and it teaches us to deal with temporary frustration through patience, perseverance, and resilience.

5. *Foster a sense of purpose and meaning:* Writing can provide you with a sense of purpose and meaning, helping you connect with your core values and passions. Even better, it can be the channel through which your passions run free and you can share them with a larger audience, leading you to a meaning that transcends your little self.

Embracing Vulnerability and Inner Discovery in the Writing Process

To fully engage in the transformative journey of writing, it's essential to embrace vulnerability and be willing to engage in your inner discovery.

This involves:

1. *Opening yourself to your emotions:* Allow yourself to feel and express your emotions as you write, creating a deeper connection with your

readers and fostering personal growth. In *Beyond Your Story*, I share my personal journey in all its facets with vulnerability and openness, not shying away even from the helplessness that was driving me to take my own life. Despite all the other stories I recount in that book, many of which are taken from real life, readers report that the parts that touched them the most are the ones where I let my emotions run free.

2. *Exploring your fears and insecurities:* Confront your fears and insecurities through your writing, using the process as an opportunity to better understand and work through these challenges. As you let them surface, see if you notice the thoughts connected to them. I found that fears, insecurities, and feelings in general are not independent entities, but byproducts of our thoughts. When we spot those thoughts, we can use our curiosity to see if they are insights or just mental constructions. Hint: if you're insecure or afraid of something, there's a good chance that some built-up thoughts are leading you. As they surface through your writing, focus on the space of possibilities beyond them, and see what's real and what's not.

3. *Being honest with yourself and your readers:* Authenticity is key to transformative writing. Be honest with yourself about your experiences, thoughts, and feelings, and share that honesty with your readers.

4. *Delving into your personal narrative:* Use writing as a means to explore your personal narrative, examining the events and experiences that have shaped your life and identity. As you look at those events, see what thoughts are scattered in your mind as you recall them. Those are the seeds that can reconnect you with any limiting belief that is constraining your experience today. Stay curious and let intuition guide you.

5. *Reflecting on your growth and progress:* Throughout your writing journey, take the time to reflect on the personal growth and progress

you've made. Acknowledge the challenges you've faced and the lessons you've learned along the way. You'll find an exercise regarding this in the prompts at the end of this chapter.

Summary

In conclusion, writing is a powerful tool for personal growth and transformation. By embracing vulnerability, cultivating authenticity, and opening up to your inner source of inspiration, you can create a writing process that is not only creative and productive but also deeply meaningful and transformative, and that not only impacts your readers but also fosters your personal growth and development. As you continue to engage in the writing process and see the implications of the Inside-Out Understanding in your life, you'll find that your work becomes more authentic, inspired, and fulfilling, reflecting the unique wisdom and perspective that only you can offer. Remember to approach your work with an open heart and an open mind, trusting that the wisdom and insights you gain will not only enrich your writing but also your life.

Exploring this Chapter's Topics:

1. Reflect on your writing journey thus far. How has writing impacted your personal growth and self-discovery? Share specific examples or experiences.

2. Discuss the concept of vulnerability in the context of your writing. Have you ever experienced a moment of vulnerability in your writing process? How did it affect your work and personal growth?

3. Consider the idea of writing as a means to explore your personal narrative. How has your writing allowed you to delve into your own life experiences and understand your identity more deeply?

Writing From Within:

1. Choose an aspect of personal growth discussed in this chapter (e.g., awareness, empathy, resilience) that resonates with you. In your next writing session, consciously focus on how your writing can facilitate growth in this area with the insights that you gain from the Inside-Out Understanding.

2. Select a fear or insecurity that you would like to explore through writing. Write a piece, either fiction or nonfiction, that addresses this fear or insecurity, aiming to better understand and work through it. As you do so, notice the thoughts that come and go as you evoke that insecurity and the events around it. See how your thoughts have guided your perception of the events, in an inside-out fashion, rather than vice versa.

3. Reflect on your writing journey by creating a timeline or journal entry detailing the challenges you've faced, the lessons you've learned, and the personal growth you've experienced. Consider how your writing has evolved over time and the ways in which it has contributed to your inner-discovery and transformation. For example, look at how your style and themes have changed as you grew and gained new experiences and insights, and notice if and how writing has become a key part of your inner discovery and personal growth.

Space for Creation

CHAPTER 8

COLLABORATING WITH TECHNOLOGY: AI AND THE INSIDE-OUT UNDERSTANDING

The rapid advancements in artificial intelligence (AI) have led to the development of powerful tools like ChatGPT, which can greatly enhance the writing process. I even dedicated an entire book and a video course to demonstrate how to use ChatGPT to unleash our writing potential while staying true to our inner voice[5]. By understanding how these tools fit within the Inside-Out Understanding, we can harness their potential while maintaining our authentic voice and creativity.

In this chapter, we'll discuss the role of AI tools like ChatGPT in the writing process and explore how the Inside-Out Understanding can inform the effective use of AI in writing, while sharing my personal stories and insights.

The Role of AI Tools like ChatGPT in the Writing Process

ChatGPT is one of the examples of how AI can support writers in streamlining their work.

ChatGPT stands for Chatbot - Generative, Pretrained, Transformer. In simple terms, it generates human-like text in response to a given question that you ask. You "feed" it a sentence, and the "transformer" component creates a coherent paragraph based on a dataset the language model has been pre-trained on. The impressive aspect is not so much the

---

[5] Tambone, Danilo, *Unleash Your Writing Potential with ChatGPT: A Comprehensive Guide for Non-Fiction Authors*, Independently published, April 10, 2023, https://www.amazon.com/Unleash-Your-Writing-Potential-ChatGPT/dp/B0C1J1LWVC

actual content with which it has been trained, but rather its ability to replicate human-like language structures, based on the patterns it has learned to recognize through various sources. In this way, when you ask ChatGPT to assist you in writing your piece and provide it with the content you want to include and the context in which you want to present it, ChatGPT organizes your writing in a clear and understandable manner. To give it a try, create a free account at https://chat.openai.com/ and use my **Creator Cheat Sheet** (available for free at https://dtamb.one/writing) to start typing in some useful prompts.

AI-powered writing tools like ChatGPT offer a range of benefits for writers, including:

1. *Idea generation:* ChatGPT can help you generate new ideas, explore diverse perspectives, and overcome writer's block by providing inspiration and creative prompts.

2. *Content organization:* AI tools can assist you in organizing your thoughts and structuring your content, making your writing more coherent and easier to follow.

3. *Editing and proofreading:* ChatGPT and other AI-powered tools can help you refine your writing by identifying grammar and punctuation errors, as well as suggesting improvements in style and readability.

4. *Efficiency and productivity:* By automating aspects of the writing process, AI tools can help you save time and boost productivity, allowing you to focus on the creative and insightful aspects of your work.

For example, with this book and the previous one, ChatGPT has assisted me in organizing my thoughts, monitoring grammar and punctuation, and suggesting improvements in style and readability, ultimately enhancing the reading experience while still preserving my unique voice.

How the Inside-Out Understanding Can Inform the Effective Use of AI in Writing

While AI tools can be immensely valuable for writers, it's essential to approach their use within the context of the Inside-Out Understanding. Here are some tips for effectively using AI in your writing process, based on my experiences:

1. *Maintain your authentic voice:* While AI tools can provide helpful suggestions and guidance, remember that your unique voice and perspective are essential to your writing. Use ChatGPT as a collaborator rather than a replacement for your own creativity. For example, when you want to improve a piece of your writing, you may enter as a prompt something like: *"Check the following piece for grammar and readability and provide an alternative if needed, still preserving my unique voice,"* followed by the text you want ChatGPT to check. Besides, I advise not to rely solely on ChatGPT to generate content, firstly because the piece would be without a soul and not contain your unique insights, and then because the tone might sound flat and monotonous. Instead, I like to provide ChatGPT with a clear description of what I want to create, I let it generate an initial draft, and then I work out the results with subsequent refinements and enhancements.

2. *Cultivate mindfulness and embrace the human-AI partnership:* As you engage with AI tools, maintain a sense of presence and awareness, ensuring that you stay in the driver's seat and remain in tune with your inner wisdom and intuition. You decide when to use AI and when to let your wisdom guide your pen on paper or your fingers on the keyboard. Sometimes I get an insight and I create a prompt for ChatGPT, I let its reply sit for a while to see where it leads me, and then I take it from there. Other times I see a more sustained dance between my insights and the outputs it generates. As it learns to follow my streams of thoughts and intuitions, it becomes like a glove and supports me, as in a partnership between my human creativity and the capabilities of the technology. It

doesn't shout, doesn't take it personally when I point out something in its content that doesn't resonate with what I feel inside and sense as true, thanks me for the insights I share with it, and gently rearranges it to suit the content to my inner knowing until I'm happy with the results. For me, this balance has created a synergy that enhances my work while preserving my authenticity.

3. *Reflect on your growth:* As you incorporate AI tools into your writing process, take time to reflect on how the technology is influencing your growth and development as a writer. Consider the ways in which it is expanding your creative horizons, as well as the lessons you're learning about maintaining your authenticity in the face of technological advancements. For me, ChatGPT has given free rein to my creativity first and foremost by giving me the chance to overcome my linguistic limitations. Being a non-native English speaker and writer, oftentimes I struggle with the proper linguistic form and my writing may sound unnatural and clunky to natives. ChatGPT has been trained specifically to create output that sounds human-like. It's like having 24/7 a linguistic assistant by my side. And, if I had human assistants very well trained on language by my side, I wouldn't delegate my creative part to them, but I would gladly ask their feedback on grammar and readability as I write. Then, I would review the results to ensure they match my message and its underlying soul. That's what I do with ChatGPT, and that's what I advise you to do as well.

Summary

In conclusion, AI tools like ChatGPT have the potential to revolutionize the writing process, offering valuable support and assistance to writers. By approaching their use within the context of the Inside-Out Understanding, you can ensure that your collaboration with technology enhances your work while preserving your unique voice and perspective. As you continue to explore the possibilities offered by AI, remember to remain mindful and true to yourself, embracing the transformative power of both technology and the human spirit.

Exploring this Chapter's Topics:

1. Discuss your current experience with AI tools like ChatGPT in the writing process. How are these tools helping or hindering your work? Share specific examples.

2. Reflect on the importance of maintaining your authentic voice when using AI tools in your writing. How can you ensure that your unique perspective and creativity are preserved while collaborating with technology?

3. Consider the idea of a human-AI partnership in writing. How do you envision a successful collaboration between human creativity and AI technology? What are the potential benefits and challenges of such a partnership?

Writing From Within:

1. Choose a writing project and use an AI tool like ChatGPT to assist you in the process. Focus on maintaining your authentic voice while incorporating the suggestions and guidance provided by the AI.

2. Practice mindfulness during a writing session that involves using an AI tool. Observe your thoughts, emotions, and reactions as you interact with the technology, ensuring that you remain in tune with your inner wisdom and intuition.

3. If you have already started using AI, reflect on your growth as a writer since incorporating AI tools into your writing process. Write a journal entry or essay discussing the ways in which AI is influencing your development and the lessons you're learning about maintaining authenticity in the face of technological advancements.

Space for Creation

CHAPTER 9

WRAPPING UP

As we reach the conclusion of this book, it's important to remember that the journey of writing from within is an ongoing process. Embracing the Inside-Out Understanding and incorporating its principles into your writing life can lead to a more fulfilling and successful writing career. In this final chapter, we'll reflect on the ongoing journey of writing from within and discuss how to continue embracing the Inside-Out Understanding for a meaningful and rewarding writing experience.

The Ongoing Journey of Writing from Within

The process of writing from within is a lifelong journey of discovery, personal growth, and creative exploration. As you continue on this path, remember to:

1. *Stay curious:* Remain open to new experiences, ideas, and insights, as they can inspire and inform your writing.

2. *Trust your inner wisdom:* Always listen to your intuition and inner guidance, as they are your most valuable sources of wisdom and inspiration.

3. *Practice mindfulness, in a broader sense:* Maintain a sense of presence and awareness in your writing and daily life, fostering a deeper connection with your authentic voice and creativity.

4. *Embrace vulnerability:* Be willing to delve into your emotions, fears, and insecurities, using the writing process as a tool for discovery and personal growth, and then notice what you sense beyond the thoughts that generated those emotions, fears, and insecurities. In that sacred space, you'll find a wellspring of creativity always ready to flow through you.

5. *Reflect on your progress:* Regularly take the time to reflect on your writing journey, acknowledging the challenges you've faced, the lessons you've learned, and the growth you've experienced.

Embracing the Inside-Out Understanding for a Fulfilling and Successful Writing Career

To continue embracing the Inside-Out Understanding in your writing career, consider the following:

1. *Cultivate a supportive writing community:* Surround yourself with like-minded individuals who share your passion for writing from within and can offer encouragement, feedback, and camaraderie. Year after year, I join the *Creating the Impossible* Program led by Michael Neill[6]. In 90 days, participants learn to see the Three Principles at work in their daily creations, discover how *impossible* is just another thought in their head, and experience life's creative force flowing through them. Most importantly, they let go of their limiting beliefs and open up to life's mystery, supporting each other on the respective journeys. I created this book, the previous one, and the one that will soon be published in that same vibrant community. The *impossible project* that each participant chooses may be absolutely anything, from writing a book to launching a course or a coaching community, from creating a piece of art to conducting an event under seemingly impossible conditions. The underlying principle, though, remains the same: when we let go of a limited self that has no idea of how to handle a future that nobody can foresee, and surrender to a creative force that is larger than us and flows through us to turn the formless into form, then we witness miracles in our life – just as it happens when we follow our wisdom and turn our insights into a published book. I have seen too many miracles happening in that community not to recommend it. For something more targeted at the writing process, see the next point.

---

[6] https://www.michaelneill.org/cti/

2. *Continue learning and growing:* Pursue opportunities for personal and professional development, whether through workshops, courses, books, or mentorship. Specifically, on the topic of book writing and publishing, I highly recommend *Hay House Writer's Community Membership*[7], which includes four different learning pathways and related online community for Beginning Writers and Aspiring, Publishing, or Promoting Authors. I appreciated the quality of their learning materials, the invaluable insights coming from one of the most outstanding and largest independent publishing companies in the world and the leading publisher in the self-help industry, its community of writers, and the chance to be selected as one of their published authors. To get a glimpse of their training content, you can follow the Program's link in the footnote and grab a copy of *The Book You Were Meant to Write*[8] by Kelly Notaras, who conducts the trainings and Q&A sessions together with Reid Tracy, CEO of Hay House.

3. *Explore new writing technologies:* Stay informed about the latest advancements in writing technology, such as AI tools like ChatGPT, and consider how they can enhance your writing process while maintaining your authentic voice.

4. *Set (un)achievable goals:* Establish clear, realistic, or even impossible goals for your writing career, and assess your progress toward achieving them. Be open to the insights you'll get along the way and see where they lead you. Instead of being carried out by thoughts and expectations and labeling yourself as a writer or an author, notice how Life flows through you, either in the form of a book or otherwise. Books are living beings. Sometimes, they require years before coming to life, or remain in draft forever. Other times, they

---

[7] https://www.hayhousewriterscommunity.com/

[8] Notaras, Kelly, *The Book You Were Meant to Write: Everything You Need to (Finally) Get Your Wisdom onto the Page and into the World,* Hay House Inc., November 13, 2018, https://www.amazon.com/Book-You-Were-Born-Write/dp/1401955606

take form effortlessly in front of your eyes and generate side opportunities you would have never expected. Stay open to Life's mystery and listen to the voice that tells in which unique way you'll turn it into matter.

5. *Celebrate your successes:* Acknowledge and celebrate your accomplishments, both big and small, as they are important milestones on your writing journey.

Summary

As you continue on your writing journey, remember that the Inside-Out Understanding offers a powerful ground for cultivating a fulfilling and successful writing career. By remaining true to yourself, embracing vulnerability and mindfulness, and fostering a deep connection with your authentic voice, you can create work that is not only creatively satisfying but also transformative for both you and your readers. Keep exploring, growing, and evolving as a writer, trusting in the wisdom of the Inside-Out Understanding to guide and inspire you every step of the way.

Exploring this Chapter's Topics:

1. Reflect on your experience of embracing the Inside-Out Understanding throughout this book. Which principles or practices have resonated with you the most? Share specific examples from your own journey.

2. Discuss the importance of staying curious, trusting your inner wisdom, and practicing mindfulness in your writing journey. How have these concepts influenced your approach to writing and personal growth?

3. Consider the role of vulnerability in your writing process. How has embracing vulnerability and inner discovery contributed to your growth as a writer? Share personal experiences or insights.

Writing From Within:

1. Seek out and join a writing community or group that shares your passion for writing from within. Engage with fellow writers, share your work, and offer support and feedback to others.

2. Set aside time each month to reflect on your writing journey. Write a journal entry or personal essay discussing your progress, challenges, and successes, as well as any insights or lessons you've learned along the way.

3. Commit to ongoing learning and growth by enrolling in workshops, courses, or reading books related to writing and personal development. Keep exploring new writing technologies and tools, such as AI applications, to enhance your writing process while staying true to your authentic voice.

4. Create a list of (un)achievable goals for your writing career, both short-term and long-term. Develop a plan for working towards these goals, regularly review and update your progress as you move forward, and remain curious of how the creative Life force takes form through you, whether in the form of a book or otherwise.

Space for Creation

A NEW BEGINNING

Congratulations on completing this transformative journey! This book has guided you through the art of writing from within, aiding you in embracing the Inside-Out Understanding and unlocking your inner wisdom to create authentic and impactful content. This holds true whether you're crafting a fiction or non-fiction book, or any other form of writing. Regardless of your writing experience, I trust this book has provided valuable insights and kindled your passion for the craft.

Remember, the journey to writing is an adventure, laden with unique challenges. However, by internalizing the Inside-Out Understanding and implementing the principles outlined in this book, you can surmount obstacles, tap into your genuine voice, and create high-quality content that deeply resonates with your readers.

As you embark on this exciting new phase of your writing life, maintain the importance of authenticity and passion as guiding lights. Allow yourself to naturally write from the heart, ensuring an honest connection with your readers. This will enable you to develop content that genuinely reflects your unique perspective and speaks to your audience.

I wish you immense success on your writing journey and encourage you to continue exploring the limitless possibilities of writing from within. Remember, your imagination is the only boundary to the extraordinary things you can accomplish!

Embrace your inner voice,
Danilo

NEXT STEPS

Thank you for taking the time to read *Writing from Within!* I hope you found the information and techniques provided in this book helpful in improving your writing skills.

If you enjoyed this book, I would be extremely grateful if you could leave an honest review on the platform where you purchased it. Your feedback is valuable to me in at least two ways: first, it helps me improve my writing and serve you better; second, book reviews can help spread the word and assist readers in finding the best book for them.

If you have any suggestions or ideas on how I can improve future editions of this book, please do not hesitate to share them with me. I would love to hear from you and implement any changes that will make the book even better.

You can reach me at www.danilotambone.com/contact.

Lastly, I have many new developments in store. If you subscribed for the **Creator Cheat Sheet**[9], you'll receive my occasional updates and new content directly in your inbox. And don't worry, I hate spam as much as you do!

Thank you again for choosing *Writing from Within*. I hope this book has inspired you to take your writing to new heights, and I look forward to seeing what you create with the help of the Inside-Out Understanding.

---

[9] https://dtamb.one/writing

BIBLIOGRAPHY

- Banks, Sydney, *The Missing Link: Reflections on Philosophy and Spirit*, Lone Pine Media Productions (B.C.) Ltd, 2021.
- Neill, Michael, *The Inside-Out Revolution*, Hay House UK, 6th edition, May 2013
- Neill, Michael, *The Space Within*, Hay House Inc, May 2016
- Neill, Michael, *Creating the Impossible: A 90-day Program to Get Your Dreams Out of Your Head and into the World*, Hay House Inc, Jan 2018
- Pransky Jack, Kelley Thomas, *How the formless comes into form: A process by which Universal Mind powers consciousness and thought to create people's psychological lives*, 27 April 2017, https://www.tandfonline.com/doi/full/10.1080/23311908.2017.1307633

ABOUT THE AUTHOR

Danilo Tambone is an Author, Transformative Coach, Agile Coach, and Scrum Master.

In the midst of his career, a profound professional and personal crisis led him to embrace change as a driving force rather than an obstacle. This transformation inspired him to assist individuals, teams, and organizations in stepping into their power and achieving personal, professional, and business success.

The discovery of the Inside-Out Understanding, particularly through the work of Transformative Coach Michael Neill, enabled him to connect the dots on how the formless turns into form.

Today, Danilo dedicates his energy to unleashing human potential, regardless of the role he takes on. His efforts have led to the publication of *Unleash Your Writing Potential with ChatGPT: a Comprehensive Guide for Non-Fiction Authors*, and now also *Writing from Within: Unleash your Creativity with the Inside-Out Understanding*.

He is currently working on his soon-to-be-published non-fiction book, *Beyond Your Story: Unleash Your Potential with the Hero's Journey and the Inside-Out Understanding* and on *AI Foundations: Discover the World of Artificial Intelligence and Begin Your Journey as an AI Whisperer*.

Meet him at danilotambone.com.

BACK COVER

In *Writing from Within: Unleash Your Creativity with the Inside-Out Understanding*, author Danilo Tambone guides you on a transformative journey to unlock your authentic voice and tap into the wellspring of creativity that lies within us all.

Drawing on the powerful insights of the Inside-Out Understanding, this book offers a unique and inspiring approach to writing that will help you deepen your connection to your inner wisdom, enhance your creative expression, and find true fulfillment as an author.

With a blend of practical advice, personal stories, and illuminating examples, *Writing from Within* will show you how to:

- Embrace the Inside-Out Understanding to create meaningful and authentic pieces of writing
- Cultivate mindfulness and presence in your writing practice
- Develop your unique writing style and voice
- Harness the power of flow to improve productivity and enjoyment in the writing process
- Nurture your intuition and insight to fuel your creativity

Whether you're an experienced author seeking to refine your craft or an aspiring writer looking for guidance on your creative journey, *Writing from Within* will provide you with the tools and inspiration you need to unleash your creative potential and become the writer you've always wanted to be.

Embark on this transformative journey today and experience the true power of writing from within.